TEN HOUSES

TEN HOUSES

Edited by Oscar Riera Ojeda

Enrique Browne

First published in the United States of America by:

Rockport Publishers, Inc.

33 Commercial Street

Gloucester, Massachusetts 01930

Telephone: 508-282-9590

Fax: 508-283-2742

Distributed to the book trade and art trade in the

United States by:

North Light, an imprint of

F & W Publications

1504 Dana Avenue

Cincinnati, Ohio 45207

Telephone: 513-531-2222

ISBN 1-56496-391-8

10 9 8 7 6 5 4 3 2 1

Cover Photo: House in San Damian Passage / Photo by Luis Poirot

Back Cover Images (left to right from the top): Pages 14, 54, 86, 31, 63, 93, 39, 74, 103, 47.

Page 2: House on Paul Harris Street, Main Entrance

Printed in Hong Kong

Graphic Design: Lucas H. Guerra / Oscar Riera Ojeda

Layout: Oscar Riera Ojeda

Contents

Foreword

by Oscar Riera Ojeda

During the past few years, the center of attention in residential architecture has seemed restricted to clearly identifiable regional examples of the main countries: English and Japanese minimalists, the spatial play of Cantón Ticino architects, Swiss and Nordic precision, and the Portuguese poetic, they seem to attract all the critical interest. However, the globalizing explosion of recent years has allowed us to discover and value other identities, some of them—such as the Mexican—with lengthy histories. Others are emerging now: the Australians, who have Glenn Marcutt as a standout figure; the Canadian contingent of Nova Scotia, led by Brian McKay Lyons; or the Chilean of the southern (Chiloé) and central (Santiago and environs) areas. In the latter region, Enrique Browne realized the totality of the ten houses selected here.

In 1982, when he co-founded the Taller América—an entity of theoretical reflection[1]—with Sergio Larraín G.M. and Cristián Fernández Cox—Enrique Browne surely did not imagine the powerful influence that this group would exercise in his country and throughout the Latin American continent. More than a decade later, it seemed ironic that this powerful intellectual explosion would proceed from Chile, a nation of fourteen million people and boxed in by its own political past, the snowy peaks of the Cordillera de los Andes, and the cold waters of the southern Pacific Ocean. Today, with democratic consolidation and a sustained economic blossoming, the nation has become a driving force in the continent.

The influence of Taller América does not simply end with theoretical labor; it also exists in the vast constructed work of its members. In both areas Enrique Browne has been a fundamental element with his numerous writings and with works such as the Snail House—which, despite being quite recent, rises as one of the most brilliant and imaginative responses to the domestic theme that Latin American architecture has lately produced. A couple of years ago, when I had the opportunity to visit this and several other houses included in this book, I was able to confirm the truth of this affirmation, which in some way extends to all of the other works.

Enrique Browne reconciles architecture and nature in these ten houses, without compromising the integrity and purity of these two often irreconcilable realities. They show his constant preoccupation to utilize, with discretion in terms of resources and independence from existing fashions, his preferred architectural tools such as the use of intermediate spaces between interior and exterior, the use of light as another material, and the emphasis on geometry. Without a doubt he has successfully exploited these elements to their maximum expression; this collection of houses is proof of that.

[1] Besides its founders, other outstanding names in Taller América include the sociologist Pedro Morandé, the poet Raúl Zurita, and architects such as Pedro Murtinho; Cristián Undurraga and Ana Luisa Devés; Luis Izquierdo and Antonia Lehmann; and Alex Moreno.

Introduction

by Enrique Browne

Adapting an old Japanese proverb, "If I explain the ten houses presented here, they are what they are. If I do not explain them, they are still what they are."[1] In other words, the works presented here should speak for themselves.

I have been fortunate to have some clients who are sensitive to the central aspects of architecture: namely, spatial quality, the play of light, and proportions. This is not so common. In fact, the majority prefer stereotypes with neutral spaces that can be decorated in any form. Formal innovation, on the other hand, initially tends to be an insult to "good taste." Thus architecture becomes a social risk—and an economical one as well—that few are disposed to take on.

Architecture should never compete with the current over-stimulation of the senses: rock music at incredible decibel levels, home theaters, computers, and so on. On the contrary, our profession is an art of subtle emotions and fine sensibilities. It is not a discipline of maximization but an art of equilibrium. Let me give an example. Someone hires an architect to design a hillside home. Obviously then, the view—the major reason for buying the site in the first place—is of maximum importance. The architect designs a home using lots of glass. The owner likes the idea, but at the same time, wants the house to have good thermal isolation. In a second version, therefore, the design includes thermopanes. The client accepts it, but adds that the house also should be as economically priced as possible. At this point, a balancing act begins: How much glass? How thermally isolated? How economical? The answers are subjective, and the architect and client will not always come to the same conclusions. But there are even more basic questions that need to be asked. "Man is more a sentimental animal than a rational one," said Unamuno. Along the same lines, a scholar once noted, "Emotions, contrary to what we think, are not merely subjective aggregates to thought, but rather the most basic characteristic of what it means to be human: the infrastructure that sustains spiritual experience and makes the perception of the world and of oneself possible. Knowledge of reality is not an exclusive function of thought, but rather requires feeling as well."[2] I can confirm this through my own experience. I am satisfied with a project

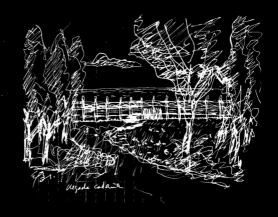

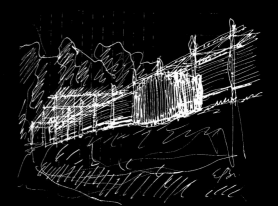

Left: *Edwards-Cosmelli 1, original version of the house (top). After modifications, the house was built as shown (left).*

Opposite Page: *Preliminary sketches of the Summer Cabin in Isla Negra.*

Refuge in Lago San Pablo, Ecuador. Plan, Section, Elevation and Perspectives

when I feel it is good, not when I know it is. I experience a sort of internal peace. Feelings are rarely wrong, unlike thoughts. Finding clients who share these feelings is indeed auspicious.

Let me add something about the physical context of the houses. Only three of them are outside Santiago, Chile. The Houses in Pirque I and II are in an agricultural area near the Maipo River. The House in Zapallar is located in a seaside resort on the Pacific Ocean, 90 miles (150 kilometers) from Santiago. With respect to the latter, a condition for the sale of the site was that the new construction must not obstruct the view of the sea from the existing house situated behind it. For this reason, the house was encrusted in the land to take advantage of the slope. This desire to insert the structure into the earth had been tried some years before in the project for the modest Cabin on San Pablo Lake (Ecuador, 1976). It also appears later in the entrance to the House on La Cumbre Street.

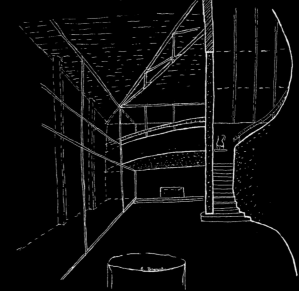

The remaining seven houses are in the country's capital, Santiago, which has some 4.5 million inhabitants. The city has a temperate climate. The Andes Mountains, with elevations of more than 16,500 feet (5,000 meters), border the city to the east. Because of its growth, the city has experienced the typical crises of metropolitan areas: congestion, pollution, etc. With each passing day, the city's inhabitants become that much more distanced from nature: the sky is no longer blue under the smog, the sound of the wind is masked by the noise of the traffic, the sunsets are the kitsch of picture postcards, and the hours of the day and even the seasons themselves are lost to the pressures of the calendar. Despite a climate that permits life in the open air almost year-round, and a population that has traditionally valued contact with nature, the foliage, the sea, and the mountains are mere memories of past vacations, when they can be afforded at all. Reclaiming these joys, therefore, is a basic aspect of each of the houses presented here.

According to Chilean tradition, in many of the houses I have emphasized the intermediate spaces—such as the interior corridor and the open-air arcade

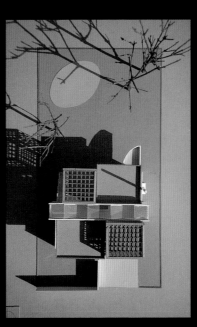

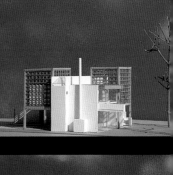

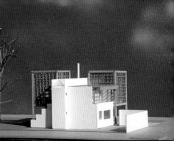

House for Sale (1983), sketch and model shots

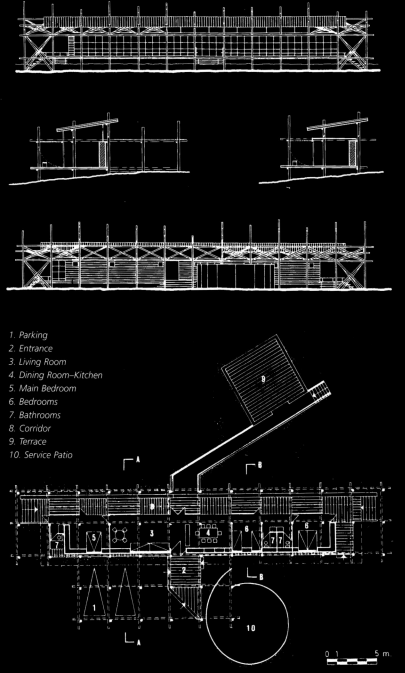

1. Parking
2. Entrance
3. Living Room
4. Dining Room–Kitchen
5. Main Bedroom
6. Bedrooms
7. Bathrooms
8. Corridor
9. Terrace
10. Service Patio

0 1   5 m.

Cabin in Isla Negra (1975), West Elevation, Sections, East Elevation, and Plan.

Chileans call the parrón—between the interiors and exteriors of the home. This idea was carried to the extreme in the Houses on Charles Hamilton Street, in which a system of brick and wooden parróns actually forms the houses. I subsequently completed a number of projects based on the same concept, but utilizing different materials. I used logs and planks in the Summer Cabin in Isla Negra (1975), for instance, and adobe and wood in the House in the Upper Reina (1976).

Another facet that appears in some of the houses (notably, the Snail House and the House on La Fuente Street) is privacy. True Santiaguinians are domestic in nature, and seek to protect their families from intruders. The walls that separate houses from their neighbors and the street is the architectonic expression of this need for privacy. Even though city ordinances have tried to convert Santiago into a "garden city" by requiring transparent frontage, Santiaguinians stubbornly have taken it upon themselves to close off their houses.

A third issue is progressive expansion, typical in Chilean houses of all social stratas. This can be seen especially in the Houses on Charles Hamilton Street, which have been tripled from their initial size, with no discernible loss to their original image. Yet another concern is coexistence with the hills: Santiago has begun to climb into the foothills of the Andes, and it is thus looking back on itself. But the majority of the houses are merely transplanted from flat land and built into brusque cuts on the slopes of the foothills. The Bilbao-Uribe House and the House on La Cumbre Street, in contrast, have been integrated into the geographical setting in a much more natural way. A final, but just as important, point to consider is the region's seismic activity, which has an obvious influence on the methods of construction.

Santiago de Chile

October 1996

[1] The Japanese proverb says "If you understand things, they are the way they are. If you do not understand them, they are still that way." In Carlos Valles, S.J., *Ligero de equipaje*, Editorial SAL TERRAE; Spain, 1987.

[2] Sergio Peña y Lillo, *El Temor y la Felicidad*, Editorial Universitaria S.A., Santiago, Chile 1989.

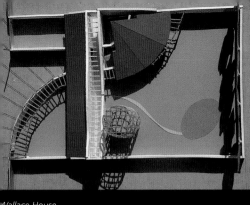

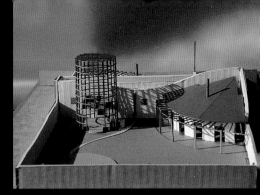

Wallace House

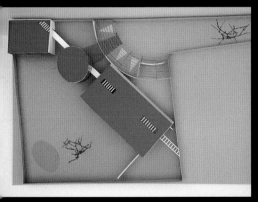

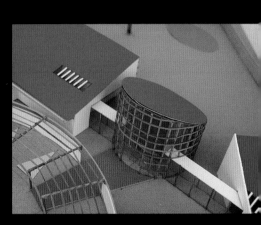

Herrera-Calvo House

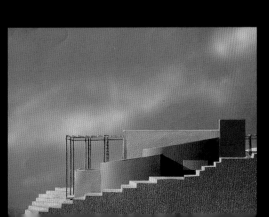

Houses on Charles Hamilton Street

Las Condes, Santiago, Chile

Above: *View from within toward a linear exterior trellis.*

Opposite Page: *A combination of brick trellises, placed every 10 feet (3 meters), run through the existing trees, which are spaced 20 feet (6 meters) apart. There is an intrinsic fusion of the building with the surrounding terrain, and a great variety of interior, interim, and exterior spaces also has been provided.*

Located in the eastern section of Santiago, two houses had to be integrated into the existing landscape while maintaining as much of existing orchards as possible. The grounds—which drop off softly toward the northwest—were planted with pear trees, aligned orthogonally every 20 feet (6 meters). A view of the Manquehue (hill) can be seen through the trees. The houses also had to be able to undergo change and expansion without disrupting the coherence or the image of the project.

In order to comply with these requirements and those of the program, the design emphasizes a division of the intermediate spaces. Both houses originated from a system of parróns based on a wooden lattice supported by brick pillars every 10 feet (3 meters), half of the distance between the trees. These parróns penetrate among the fruit trees and form the exterior spaces of the project. Their partial or total closure gives rise to the interior spaces, creating a range of environments that assist in the transition from the interior toward the exterior (living spaces, corridors, parking spaces, parrones, and others). This system also easily absorbs changes and expansion.

The houses are constructed entirely of exposed brick. The system of parróns is also the basis for the system of construction. The pillars are constructed of machine-made bricks, and encase four 4-inch (10-centimeter) bars of steel. On top of the pillars, there are longitudinal 4-by-10-inch (10-by-25-centimeter) wooden beams, over which are mounted a 2-by-8-inch (5-by-20-centimeter) lattice. The window sashes form delicate, squared membranes of wood. All of the materials are visible. The differences between the two homes arise from the necessities and preferences of each owner.

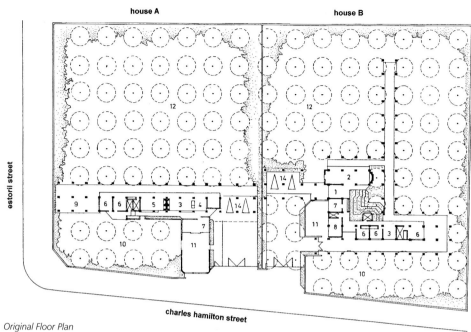

house A   house B

Original Floor Plan

estoril street

charles hamilton street

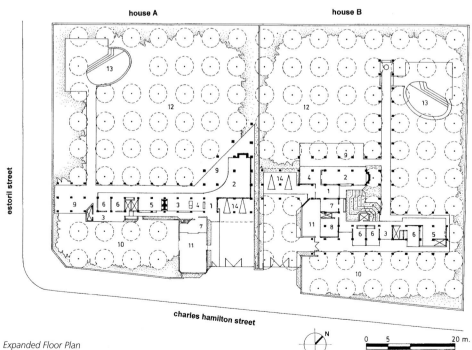

house A   house B

Expanded Floor Plan

estoril street

charles hamilton street

1. Entrance Hall
2. Living Room
3. Den
4. Dining Room
5. Main Bedroom
6. Bedroom
7. Kitchen
8. Service Bedroom
9. Terrace
10. Children's Patio
11. Service Patio
12. Garden Patio
13. Pool
14. Garage

N

0   5   20 m.

Left: *(Top) This covered terrace conforms to one of the various extensions added to the dwellings, doubling its original surface area without greatly altering the original appearance of the houses. There is a notable tendency in Chile to build on house extensions, regardless of the socio-economic standing of the occupants. (Bottom) Trellises, covered terraces, and living room. Note the subtle gradation between the interior, semi-interior, and exterior spaces of the dwelling.*

Opposite Page: *Views of and toward the central patio.*

Section C-C

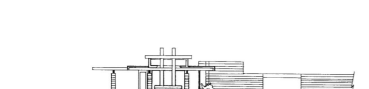

Section D-D

Section E-E

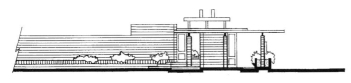

Left: *Aspects of the brick columns with wooden beams, both within and without the house. All of the different elements are exposed, expressing their structural function as well as showing off their natural color.*

Opposite Page: *View of the trellis from the interior of the domicile.*

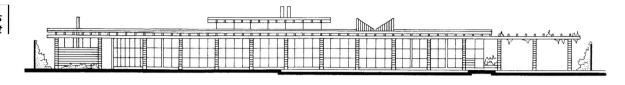

North Elevation (House A)

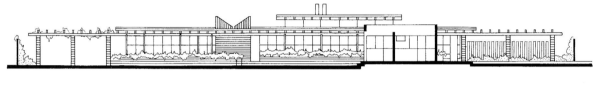

South Elevation (House A)

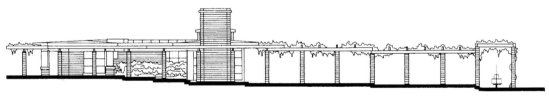

East Elevation (House B)

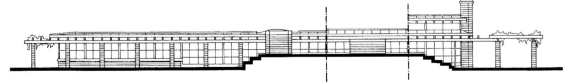

Central Courtyard Extended Elevation (House B)

Left: *(Top) Plants are an important feature within the dwelling. (Bottom) The living room is separated from the main bedroom by a double chimney.*

Opposite Page: *The partition between interior and exterior is attained by floor-to-ceiling windows, made up of delicate wooden frames.*

Right: (Top) View from the living room toward a covered terrace. (Bottom) House A. One of the extensions added to this dwelling was a new living room, running perpendicular to the lineal axis of the original. To highlight the continuity between old and new, the crystal membrane is curved, following the change of axis. The exterior consists of a covered terrace.

Opposite Page: The chimney stack also serves as the main support for the system of trellises that spread out from the central courtyard.

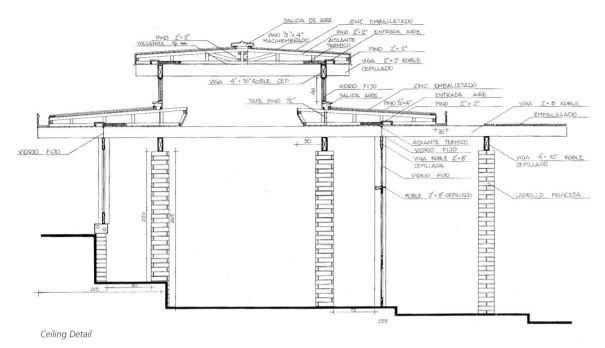

PINO 2"× 2"
VOLCANITA 16 mm
SALIDA DE AIRE
PINO 1/2"× 4" MACHIEMBRADO
ZINC EMBALLETADO
PINO 2"× 2" ENTRADA AIRE
AISLANTE TERMICO
PINO 2"× 2"
VIGA 2"× 2" ROBLE CEPILLADO
VIGA 4"× 10" ROBLE CEP.
VIDRIO FIJO
SALIDA AIRE
ZINC. EMBALLETADO
ENTRADA AIRE
PINO 2"× 2"
VIGA 2× 8 ROBLE
EMPALILLADO
TAPA PINO 1/2"
PINO 1/2"× 4"
VIDRIO FIJO
AISLANTE TERMICO
VIDRIO FIJO
VIGA ROBLE 2"× 8" CEPILLADA
VIDRIO FIJO
ROBLE 2"× 8" CEPILLADO
VIGA 4"× 10" ROBLE CEPILLADO
LADRILLO PRINCESA

40
220
265
50
20
225   80
75
225

Ceiling Detail

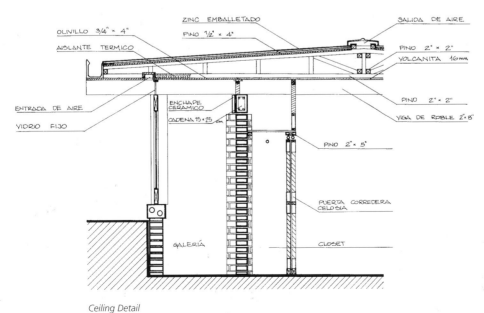

OLIVILLO 3/4"× 4"
AISLANTE TERMICO
ZINC EMBALLETADO
PINO 1/2"× 4"
SALIDA DE AIRE
PINO 2"× 2"
VOLCANITA 16 mm
PINO 2"× 2"
VIGA DE ROBLE 2"× 8"
ENTRADA DE AIRE
VIDRIO FIJO
ENCHAPE CERAMICO
CADENA 15× 25 cm
PINO 2"× 5"
PUERTA CORREDERA CELOSIA
GALERÍA
CLOSET

Ceiling Detail

House on Paul Harris Street

Las Condes, Santiago, Chile

The 89-by-257-foot (27-by-78-meter) lot is located in the eastern part of Santiago, oriented on the north-south axis. There are large pine trees at the back of the property, and the Andes Mountains can be seen to the east. The house is located at the center of the lot in order to maximize the views surrounding the lot. Designed on two levels, the first level of the house is for public spaces, the second for private.

Dividing walls border the lot, as the location of the house created two open zones to the south and the north. The north end of the lot also is divided in half by an entrance parrón. Three patios were thus formed: an entrance patio, a front patio, and a patio-garden to the south. The house was developed from a tall and elongated central space, reconciled by two parallel wall-beams. This space vents sun to the southern areas of the house and concentrates horizontal and vertical circulation. The covering is made of thermopanes to avoid heat loss. An undulating lower wall provides a counterpoint to the geometric rigidity of the wall-beams. This contemporary version of the central patio serves as a nucleus for the whole composition. Similarly, two roofs and two pergolas adhere with an inverted geometry on both sides.

The closure of the house is independent of the described volumes. It consists of a continuous line of glass that zigzags freely between the walls and the pillars, forming two diverse internal and intermediate spaces. The house thus acquires layers, leaving "spaces within spaces." The interior-exterior gradation also is expressed in the plasticity of the house. The intermediate spaces are the most figurative. They have controlled vegetation, red tones of wood in the ceilings, and brick in the flooring. Outside, the green of the trees and the colors of the mountains are the noticeable elements. This play between figure and abstraction is evident in the elevations: the frontal facades tend toward the figure, while the lateral facades tend toward abstraction.

SITE PLAN
1. Entrance Patio
2. Garden Patio
3. Pool

FIRST FLOOR PLAN
1. Entrance Hall
2. Dining Room
3. Living Room
4. Kitchen
5. Service Bedroom
6. Laundry
7. Pergola
8. Office-Bedroom

SECOND FLOOR PLAN
9. Bedrooms
10. Studio
11. Children's Study
12. Terrace

paul harris street

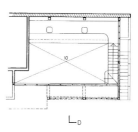

Third Floor Plan

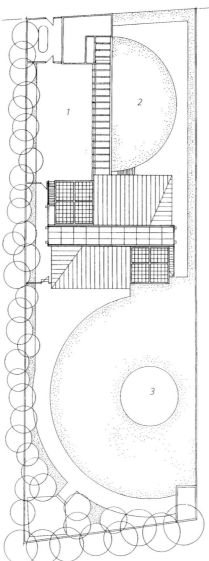

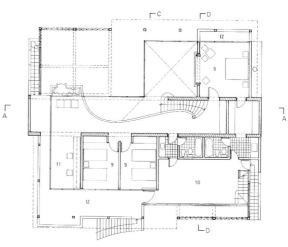

Second Floor Plan

First Floor Plan

0 1 2 3m.

Left: *A creeper plant—whose leaves turn red and yellow in autumn—covers the pergola.*

Opposite Page: *(Top) Trellised entrance to the house. (Bottom) To enter the dwelling, one needs to make a double turn, passing through this minimal space.*

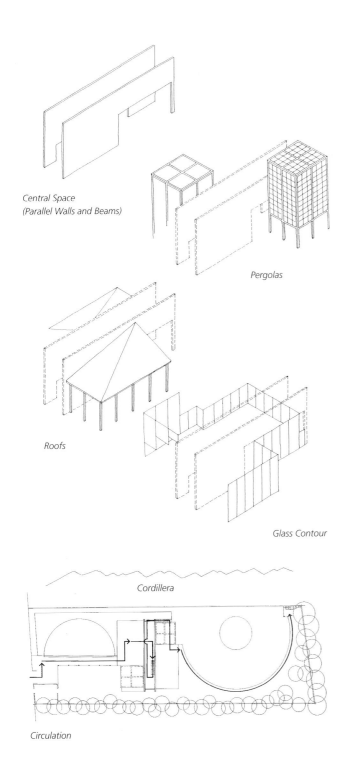

Central Space
(Parallel Walls and Beams)

Pergolas

Roofs

Glass Contour

Cordillera

Circulation

Left: (Top) The western and eastern sides of the house, which face toward the neighbors, are closed off. (Center) This stairway leads from the central corridor toward the garden pergola. (Bottom) The partition between interior and exterior spaces is achieved by a crystal membrane, which winds between ceilings and pergolas. As such, the partition is notably discreet in appearance.

Opposite Page: The front-facing pergola shields a window-lined, informal living room.

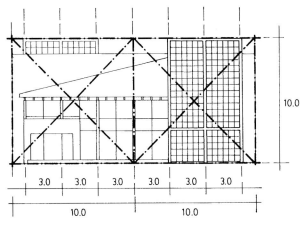

Geometric Regulation-Elevation

3.0 3.0 3.0 3.0 3.0 3.0

10.0 10.0

10.0

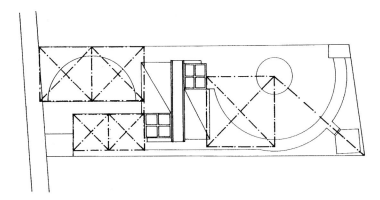

Geometric Regulation-Exteriors

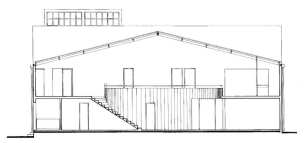

Longitudinal Section A-A

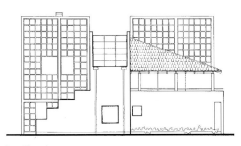

East Elevation

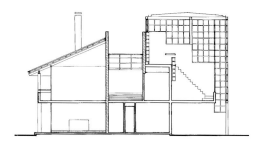

Transversal Section D-D

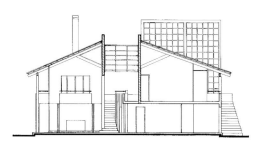

Transversal Section C-C

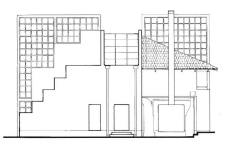

West Elevation

Right: (Top) View of the living room and the main bedroom. The stairway to the first floor is on the right. (Bottom) Views of the glass-roofed main hallway.

Opposite Page: The outer curve of the corridor passes through the glass partition, entering into the pergola.

The different spatial situations can be appreciated by an "architectonic walk," which begins in the main entrance door and ends at a pergola with a fountain at the rear of the grounds. Because of its inverted geometry, the house seems to turn round as the walker advances.

The pergolas and the other intermediate spaces increase the volume of the house. The proportions of the plans and the elevations are accomplished both in the house and in the exteriors. A 10-foot (3-meter) module was adopted for such effects.

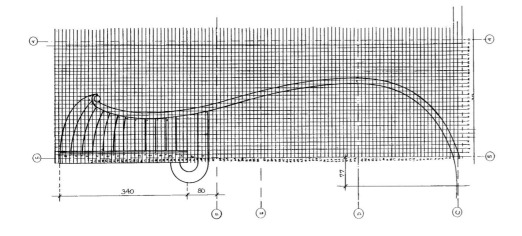

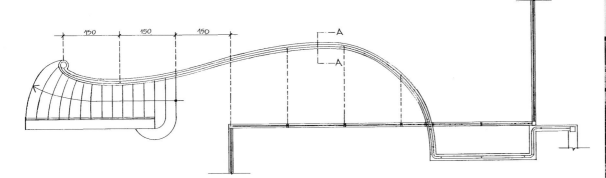

Handrail and Staircase Outline

PROY. PATAS CENTRAL

$\frac{M}{2}$ CORTE B-B

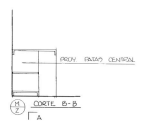

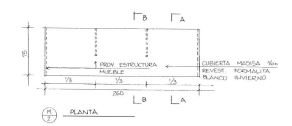

75

↑ PROY. ESTRUCTURA
MUEBLE

CUBIERTA MASISA 16m
REVEST. FORMALITA
BLANCO INVIERNO

1/3   1/3   1/3

260

$\frac{M}{2}$ PLANTA

75
45   30

FONDO MURO

CUBIERTA Y DIVISIONES
MASISA 16mm REVEST.
FORMALITA BLANCA

PROY PATAS LATERALES

D2

30   15

$\frac{M}{2}$ CORTE A-A

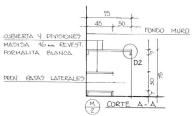

CUBIERTA MASISA 16mm.

REVEST. FORMALITA BLANCA
ARISTA A 45°

BORDE ALAMO 1"×2" CEP

FRENTE CAJON EUCALIPTUS
1"×4" ELABORADO

PROYECCION SACADO
RADIO = 4 CMS.

FONDO CAJON
TERCIADO 6mm.

D1

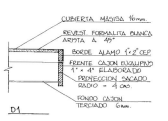

CUBIERTA MASISA 16mm

REVEST. FORMALITA BLANCA ARISTA 45°

BORDE ALAMO 1"×3" CEP

D2

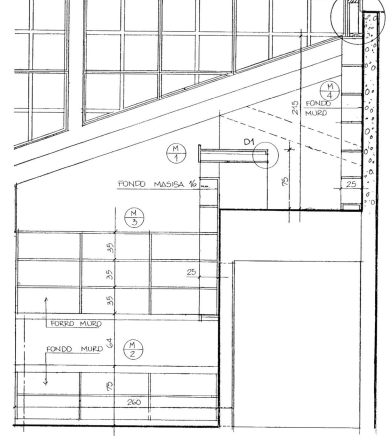

B   A

CUBIERTA MASISA 16m
REVEST. FORMALITA
BLANCO INVIERNO

$\frac{M}{4}$

215   FONDO
MURO

$\frac{M}{1}$ D1

FONDO MASISA 16 mm.

$\frac{M}{3}$

75

25

35

25

35

35

FORRO MURO

FONDO MURO

64    $\frac{M}{2}$

75

260

Studio Furniture Details

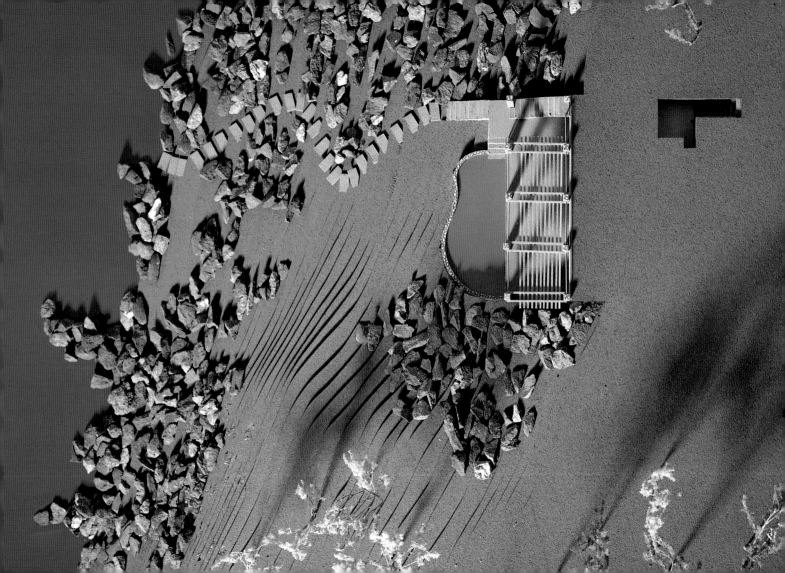

Summer House in Zapallar

Zapallar, Chile

This summer home on the Pacific coast occupies a lot of land in front of a two-story house. It was a condition for the sale of the lot that the new house should not obstruct the views of the sea from the existing house. The decision was made to submerge the new residence at the edge of a rocky cliff that reaches to the ocean. In this way, the roof is a continuation of the garden-terrace above.

The house occupies the whole front of the terrain, with spectacular views of the sea. One descends to the house by a stairway that overlooks an English patio with a water collector. The service areas abut the interior side, freeing the western edge for living spaces, such as the living room and bedrooms. The house has a great deal of functional flexibility. Two beds used as sofas in the living room can be separated by curtains to accommodate guests. The second bedroom also serves as accommodations or as an office for the owner of the house.

The living room and bedrooms overlook a terrace with a lawn that is partially covered by a horizontal blind of bamboo-like slats that offer protection from the western sun. This blind goes around the superior axis and serves to protect the house when it is not in use. From the terrace, one can descend toward a pool formed on the rocks, or directly toward the sea.

The double-helix of pillars that virtually delimits the superior and inferior terraces appears to be made of hammered concrete, in order to convey the idea of a strength. On the stairs, around the pool, and for other external elements, stones from the site were used to mimic the house's immediate natural surroundings.

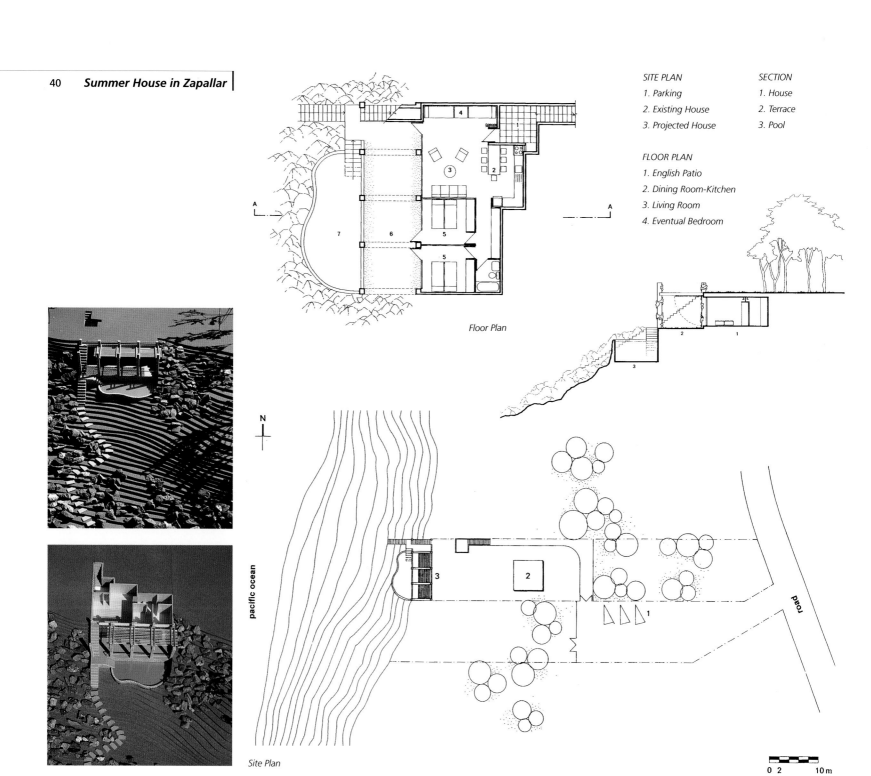

SITE PLAN
1. Parking
2. Existing House
3. Projected House

SECTION
1. House
2. Terrace
3. Pool

FLOOR PLAN
1. English Patio
2. Dining Room-Kitchen
3. Living Room
4. Eventual Bedroom

Floor Plan

pacific ocean

road

Site Plan

0 2   10 m

Left: *The house viewed from the sea. The rocks used in the construction came from the same location.*

Opposite Page: *The house is encrusted into the surrounding rock. Aerial view of the house without its garden roof.*

Right: (Top) From behind, the house looks like a balcony overlooking the horizon. (Bottom) View of the model showing the blend of architecture with the surrounding environment.

Opposite Page: View of the model without its surrounding terrain.

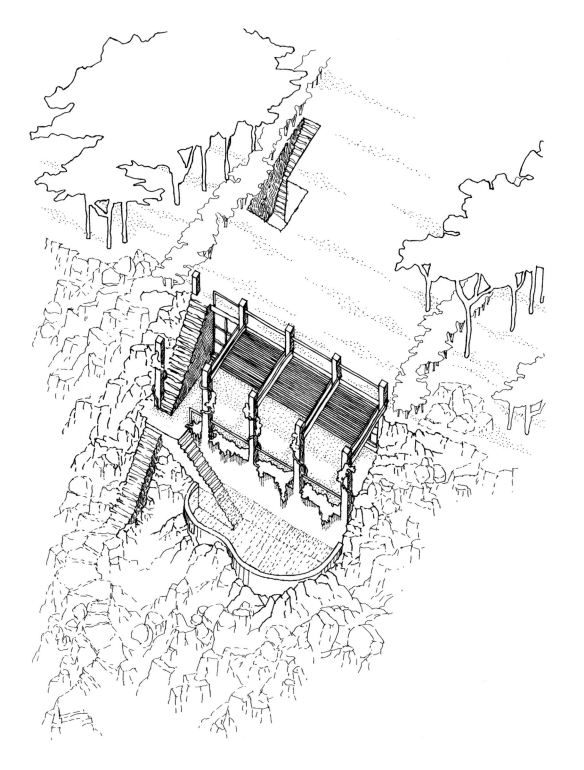

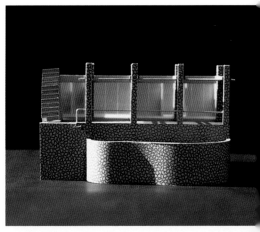

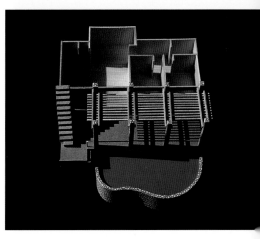

House on La Fuente Street

Las Condes, Santiago, Chile

Above: *Overhead walkway, connecting the study with an elevated patio.*

Opposite Page: *The house is cut off from public view, assuring the family's privacy. The entrance to the house is found between the tower and the perimeter walls.*

The terrain has an eastern view toward the Andes Mountains. Sunlight streams in from the same direction, as well as from the north. The owners also wanted to protect the family's privacy. The site was surrounded a high masonry wall; this closure opens onto the sloping street, where two walls turn back perpendicularly on distinct axes. The entrance patio also opens in this manner.

A semi-public zone splits off in front of the private area of the house. For the same reason, a high hermetic wall crosses the terrain, parallel to the street. This wall serves as the backbone of the house. Inside, bathroom and kitchen services align along this wall with consequent economy in the installation. This wall does not have windows, but natural overhead illumination is achieved by means of a shift back in the inferior part of the wall.

A parrón with pillars of asbestos-cement and wooden beams above abuts the wall, crossing over into the parking zone. This parrón establishes an orthogonal scheme that gives rise to a double geometry with respect to the wall parallel to the street. The partial or total closure of the parrón forms a variety of open, intermediate, or closed spaces (such as terraces, parking, and the dining room). The limits of the interior spaces follow the modulation of the parrón and have setbacks to adapt to the supporting wall. For the same reason, the areas have an east and north orientation, therefore obtaining the best views and sunlight. Three volumes establish a vertical counterpoint to the horizontality of the parrón. One corresponds to the living room; another to the father's study-library, located in the front part. This volume of two levels is joined by means of a bridge to the third level. The children's bedrooms are beneath the third level; the upper part houses a patio-terrace. In the future, this patio-terrace could remain as is, or it could be converted into more bedrooms. The union of the two volumes (study-library with children's bedrooms) delimits a small patio on the southwestern side. It also establishes the entrance axis of the house.

GROUND FLOOR PLAN
1. Entrance Patio
2. Parking
3. Entrance
4. Hall
5. Living Room
6. Dining Room
7. Kitchen
8. Service Bedroom
9. Den
10. Library
11. Bedroom
12. Main Bedroom
13. Dressing Room
14. Patio
15. Garden Patio
16. Pool
17. Storage-Changing Rooms

SECOND FLOOR PLAN
18. Office
19. Terrace Patio

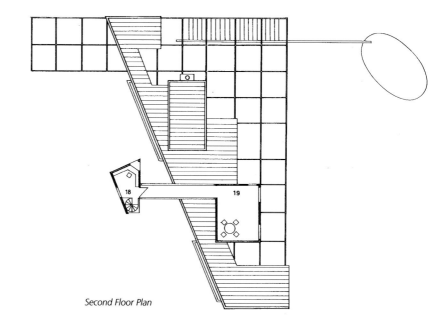

Second Floor Plan

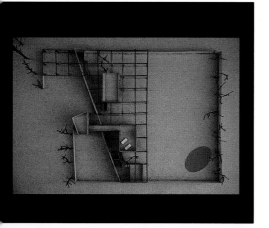

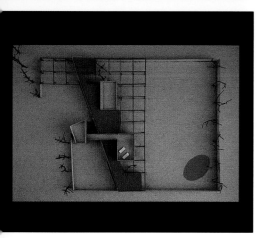

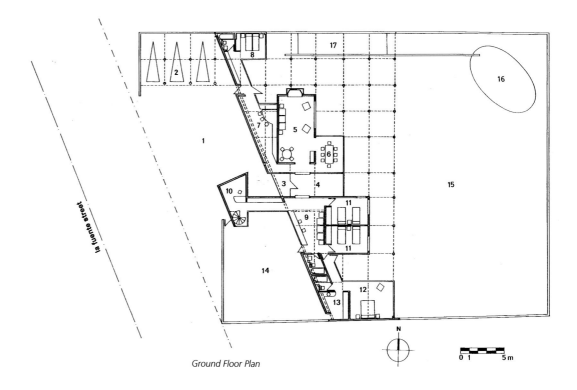

Ground Floor Plan

Left: *(Top) The Andes Mountains appear in the background. (Bottom) Views of the tower and the entrance.*

Opposite Page: *Overhead view of the model.*

Right: (Top) View of the front patio, with a stairway leading to the library. The overhead walk leads to the upper patio. (Bottom) View of the trellis running toward the garden.

Opposite Page: Dining room and access area to the house.

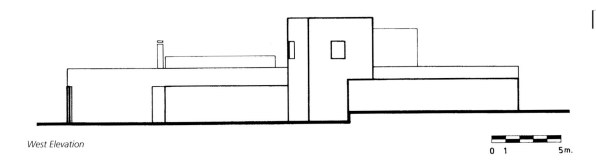

West Elevation

0   1   5 m.

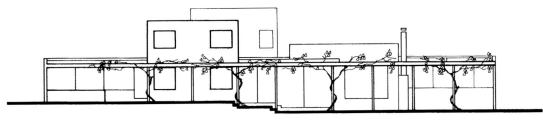

East Elevation

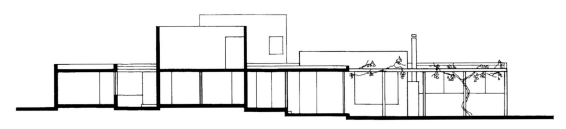

Longitudinal Section

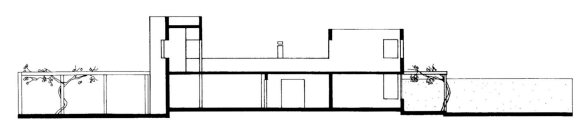

Transversal Section

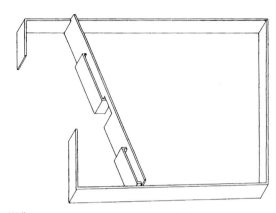

Walls

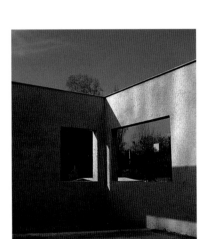

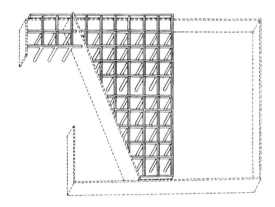

Parrón

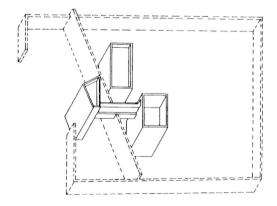

Volumes

0 1   5m.

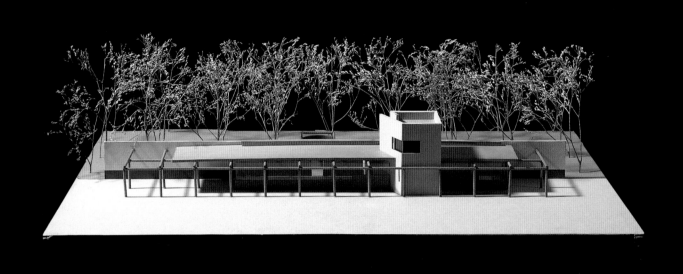

House in Pirque (Version I)

Cruceral, Pirque, Chile

This economical weekend house outside of Santiago rests on a lot with tiered terraces that descend northward toward the canyon of the Maipo River. The terrain is almost flat and the river can't be seen until the beginning of the last 99 feet (30 meters) of the lot. The owners wanted to use two-thirds of the land for planting, leaving the third at the riverside for the house itself. The architects proposed a large wall which cuts the plot perpendicularly. This divides the agricultural area from the residential area: the clear delineation of zones is very common in rural areas in the central part of the country.

The agricultural part of the terrain would be occupied with fruit trees (planted every 21 feet (6.4 meters). The access road would pass between them, ending in a rotunda next to the wall.

The house itself is attached to the perpendicular wall and has the best views of the river and the mountains. It consists of a parrón of cylinders, moduled at 11 feet (3.2 meters) (half of the distance between the fruit trees). Part of the parrón is covered. An independent line of windows borders the interior areas. A volume of two floors crosses the parrón, dividing the combined kitchen-dining room-living room from the office. This volume establishes a vertical counterpoint with the large wall, and concentrates the service areas in its first level. The main bedroom is on the second level, and offers spectacular panoramic views.

In the future, the house will be used year-round. Given its modularity, the house can grow without altering its aesthetic. This growth could be realized by adding bedrooms toward the western side.

Above: *A long wall separates the house from the adjoining orchard. The wall is painted in colors commonly used in country houses of the region.*

Opposite Page: *Views of the model, from both the garden and orchard sides.*

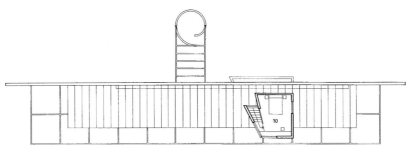

Second Floor Plan

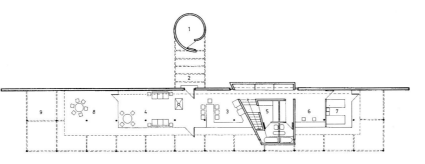

First Floor Plan

SITE PLAN
1. Caretaker's House
2. Parking
3. Fruit Trees
4. Garden
5. Pool
6. Maipo River Canyon

GROUND AND SECOND FLOOR PLAN
1. Service Patio
2. Entrance
3. Kitchen-Dining Room
4. Living Room
5. Dressing Room and Bathroom
6. Study
7. Bedroom
8. Covered Terrace
9. Parrón
10. Main Bedroom

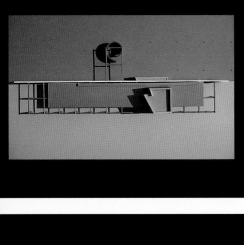

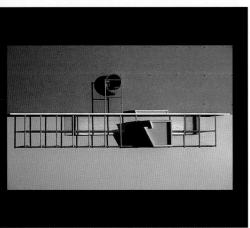

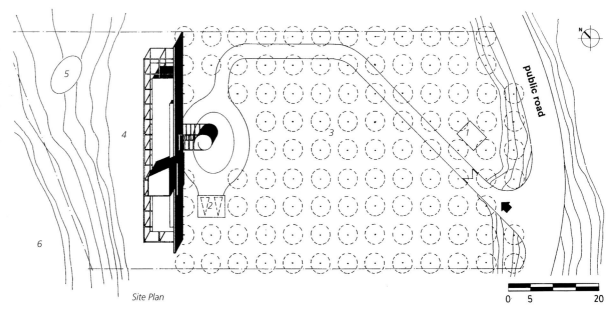

Site Plan

0   5   20

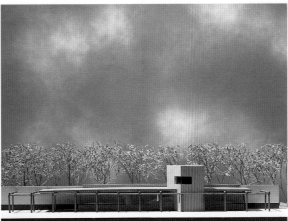

Left: *(Top) Side view of the house. (Bottom) Front and rear views of the model.*

Opposite Page: *(Top) Overhead view of the model with roof. (Bottom) Overhead view of the model without roof.*

Right: *(Top) The main bedroom is found within the tower. A trellis is supported by the longitudinal wall, its partial or total covering giving way to the intermediate and interior spaces of the house. (Bottom) View of the house from the orchard entrance.*

Opposite Page: *Overhead view of a preliminary version of the model.*

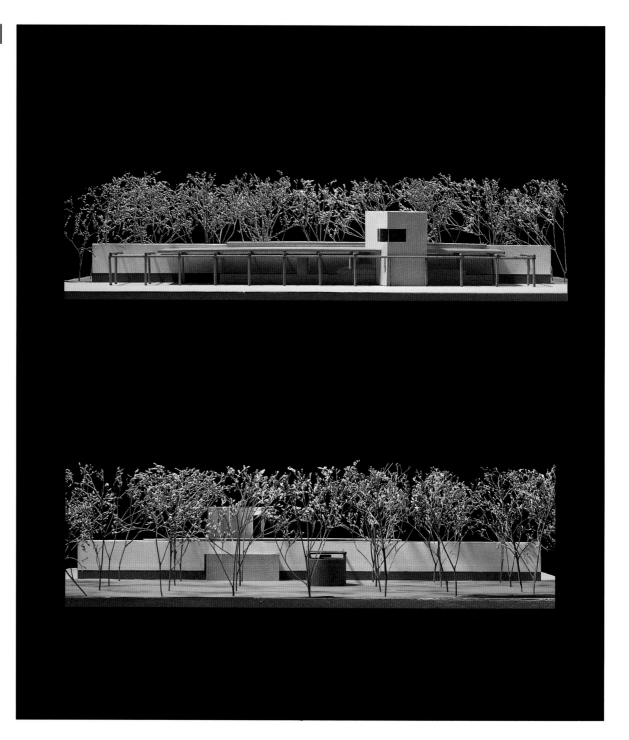

With the parrón toward the north, the thermal regulation of the house was taken care of. Primary vegetation would be deciduous leaves, controlling the sunlight during the different seasons of the year. The large and hermetic southern wall absorbs the heat that penetrates from the north, avoiding heat loss during the winter. Also, the large windows are fixed and contain ledges of wood with insulation.

The house would have walls of masonry-reinforced stucco. Given the dusty nature of the land, the walls would be painted; a natural overhead light would illuminate the large southern wall.

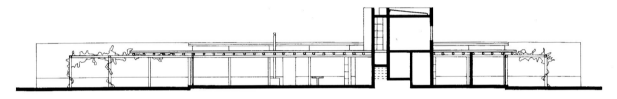

Longitudinal Section

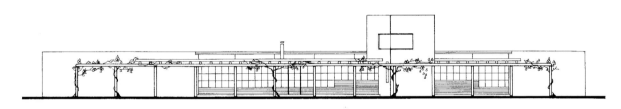

North Elevation

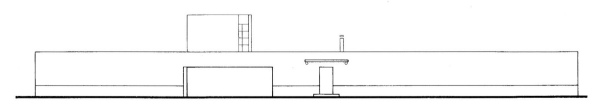

South Elevation

0 1   5m

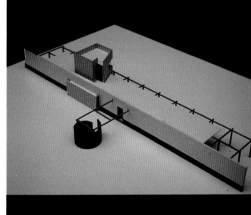

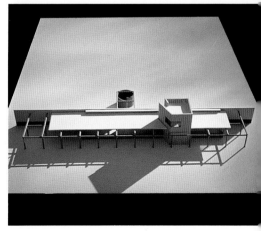

House in Pirque (Version II)

Cruceral, Pirque, Chile

Above: *The house viewed from the garden.*

Opposite Page: *Side view of house. To the left is a trellis that crosses the entire grounds. To the right is the trellis that protects the house from the northwestern sunshine.*

The house is located in a rural terrain of 55,555 square feet (5,000 square meters) beside the canyon of the Maipo River. A large transverse parrón divides the agricultural area from the residential area. The house itself is attached to the parrón in such a way that there is a pergola for both the pool and the parking area. The latter, along with a planned greenhouse, are not yet constructed.

The simple house consists of two areas: a bedroom-study and the combined kitchen-dining room-living room.

These spaces are separated by the zone of the bathroom and a circular enclosed entrance space. This area serves as a spot for leaving coats and hats, cleaning shoes, and other acts of the transition between the rural and the residential.

The interior of the house closes completely toward the south side of the terrain, which is planted with fruit trees. Closets, beds, and other things break up a structurally economical wall.

A covered terrace with an arbor of deciduous plants extends the visual area of the house that opens northward toward the canyon of the Maipo. The south wall and the arbored north compel the house to function well thermally.

Over the years, the trees in the orchard have grown considerably, covering up the house from the entrance onwards. The same has happened with the plant creepers, which have covered the trellises which surround the small construction. House and vegetation blend together presenting an ever changing appearance according to the season.

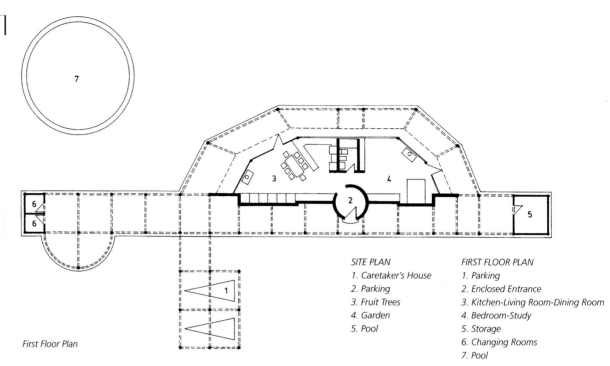

First Floor Plan

SITE PLAN
1. Caretaker's House
2. Parking
3. Fruit Trees
4. Garden
5. Pool

FIRST FLOOR PLAN
1. Parking
2. Enclosed Entrance
3. Kitchen-Living Room-Dining Room
4. Bedroom-Study
5. Storage
6. Changing Rooms
7. Pool

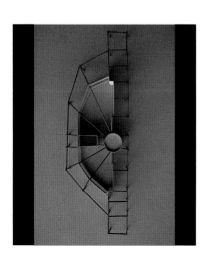

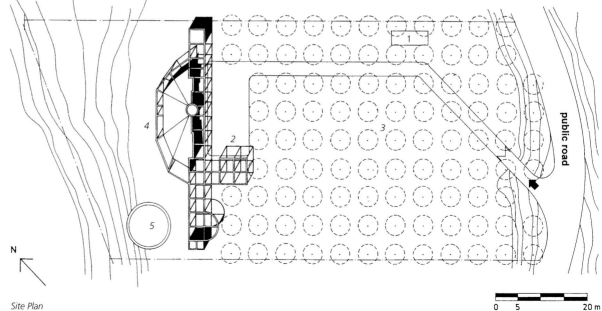

N

Site Plan

public road

0   5   20 m

Left: *(Top) Side view of house. (Bottom) When covered by a variety of creeper plants, the trellises surround the little construction, anchoring it firmly to the surrounding terrain.*

Opposite Page: *Overhead view of the model without roof.*

Right: (Top) Entrance chamber from the orchard. (Bottom) These photographs of the trellises were taken shortly after construction terminated.

Opposite Page: View of a longitudinal trellis.

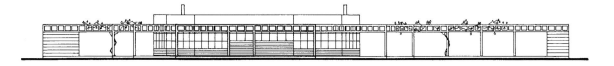

North Elevation

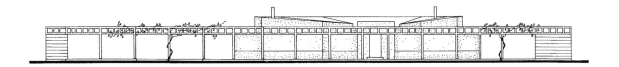

South Elevation

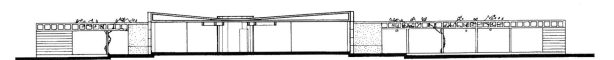

Longitudinal Section

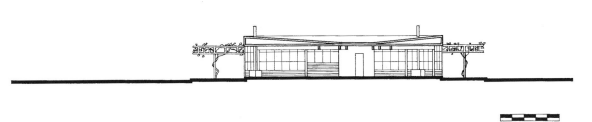

Longitudinal Section

0 1   5 m.

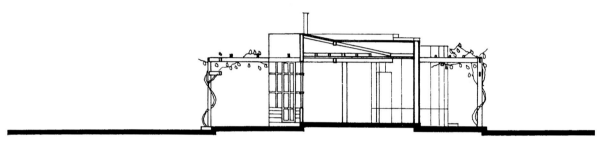

Transversal Section

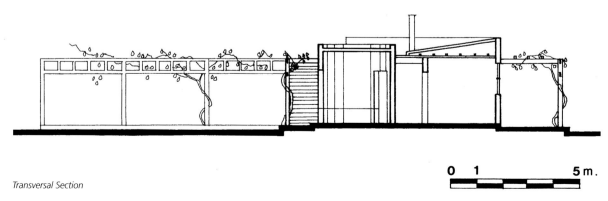

Transversal Section

0   1   5 m.

Snail House

Las Condes, Santiago, Chile

Above: *The steps make up for the difference of height between the outer and inner spiral.*

Opposite Page: *The spiral of the "snail" design resolves in a waterfall over the pool.*

The essence of patios forms the basis for the design of this house. The owners sought a dwelling that would form an indissoluble unity with the terrain. The house would not "be in" the site; rather, it would "be" the site. For this reason, the construction of the dividing wall between the Snail House and its neighbors was the first architectonic decision.

The site was almost square. The best views and sunlight were on the northern diagonal toward the street. This diagonal became the axis of the whole composition. The common areas (dining room and living room) were separated from the private spaces (bedrooms and service areas) and located in the center of the terrain, forming their own site. It started as a more compact form: a circle. Upon adjusting this space on the diagonal, an oval was formed. Given that the dining room and kitchen do not require bathrooms, the oval was left at the height of the natural terrain, 4 feet (1.2 meters).

The detached private areas (parents' bedroom, children's bedroom, and service areas) are located between the oval and the square of the dividing wall. These units form small patios and are left at street level, so as to connect bathrooms and kitchens to the public services (water and sewage).

Conceptually unifying the different parts of the house was an important part of the program. A spiral circulating around the oval achieved that unifying essence. The wall that forms the spiral begins in the entranceway and ends in a waterfall over the pool. Certain technical items, including the stairs to the roof, the boiler, and television and radio antennas are concentrated in a metallic tower on the back patio and over the axis in diagonal.

The house is white but it is painted with natural overhead light. In the gallery, the light is white, while in the dining room (the symbolic nucleus), it is yellow. There is a cut in the roof that illuminates the covered terrace beside the living room with blue light.

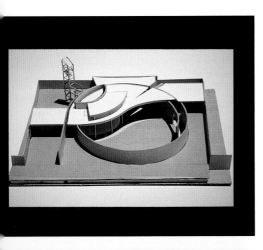

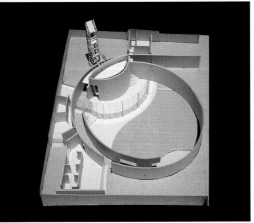

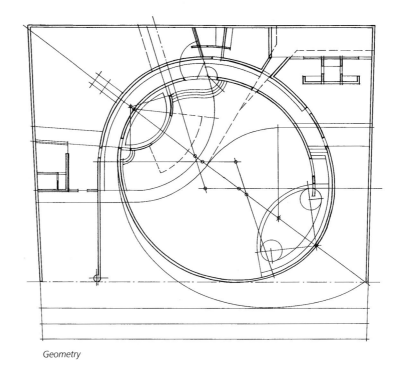

Geometry

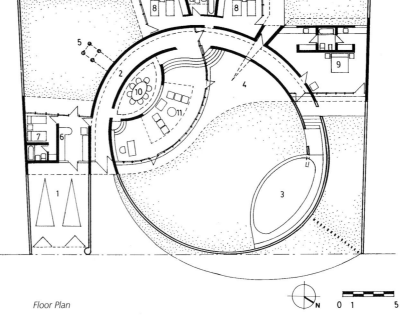

Floor Plan

1. Parking
2. Gallery
3. Pool
4. Covered Terrace
5. Mechanical Tower
6. Kitchen
7. Service Quarters
8. Bedroom
9. Parents' Bedroom
10. Dining Room
11. Living Room

N   0 1   5

Right: (Top) Daytime view of the patio-garden, seen from the covered terrace. (Bottom) Views of water falling into the pool.

Opposite Page: (Top) View of the house from the pool. (Bottom) Covered terrace.

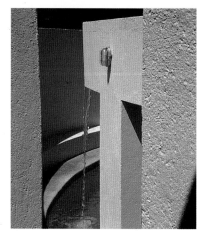

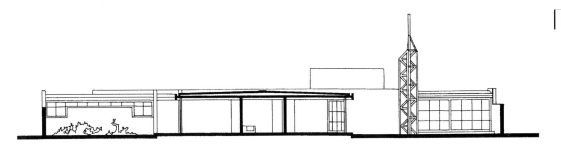

Longitudinal Section

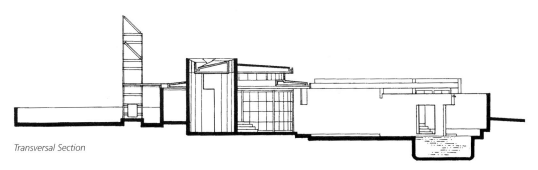

Transversal Section

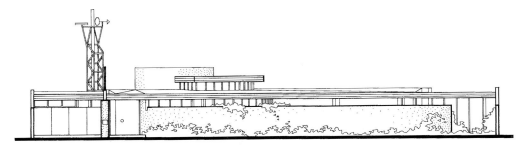

Street Elevation

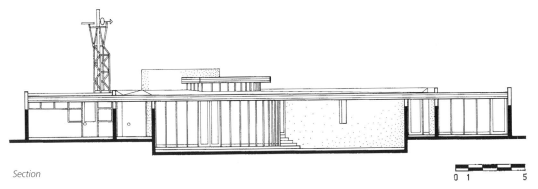

Section

0 1   5

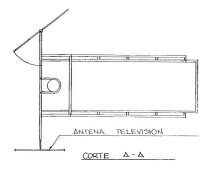

CORTE A-A

PUENTE EST. MET. SOBRE
EST. Fe [40 × 40 mm.

CHIMENEA Fe ≈ ø 10"
SEGUN ESPECIFICACION

CORTE B-B

Installation Tower Details

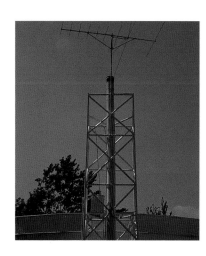

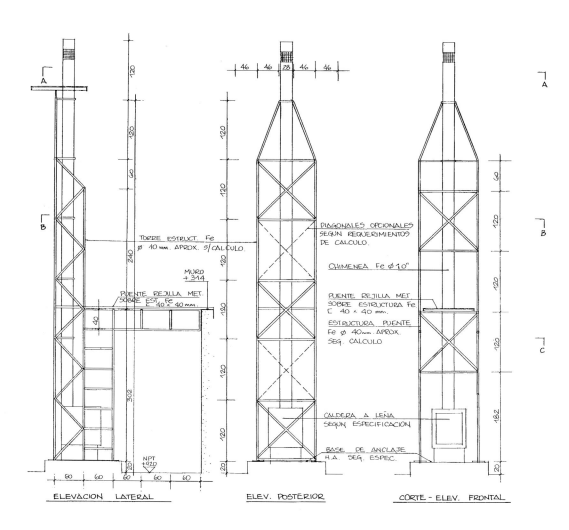

ANTENA TELEVISION

TORRE ESTRUCT. Fe
ø 10 mm. APROX. S/CALCULO.

MURO
+ 3.14

PUENTE REJILLA MET.
SOBRE EST. Fe 40 × 40 mm.

NPT
+0.20

ELEVACION LATERAL

DIAGONALES OPCIONALES
SEGUN REQUERIMIENTOS
DE CALCULO.

CHIMENEA Fe ø 10"

PUENTE REJILLA MET.
SOBRE ESTRUCTURA Fe
[40 × 40 mm.

ESTRUCTURA PUENTE
Fe ø 40mm. APROX.
SEG. CALCULO

CALDERA A LEÑA
SEGUN ESPECIFICACION

BASE DE ANCLAJE
H.A. SEG. ESPEC.

ELEV. POSTERIOR

CORTE - ELEV. FRONTAL

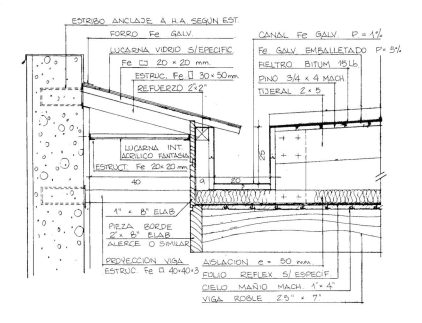

ESTRIBO ANCLAJE A H.A. SEGÚN EST.
FORRO Fe GALV.
LUCARNA VIDRIO S/EPECIFIC.
Fe ☐ 20 × 20 mm.
ESTRUC. Fe ☐ 30 × 50 mm.
REFUERZO 2"× 2"

CANAL Fe GALV. P = 1%
Fe GALV. EMBALLETADO P= 5%
FIELTRO BITUM. 15 Lb.
PINO 3/4 × 4 MACH.
TIJERAL 2 × 5

LUCARNA INT.
ACRILICO FANTASIA
ESTRUCT. Fe 20× 20 mm.
40

9   20   25

1" × 8" ELAB.
PIEZA BORDE
2"× 8" ELAB
ALERCE O SIMILAR

PROYECCION VIGA
ESTRUC. Fe ☐ 40×40×3

AISLACION e = 50 mm.
FOLIO REFLEX S/ ESPECIF.
CIELO MAÑIO MACH. 1"× 4"
VIGA ROBLE 2.5" × 7"

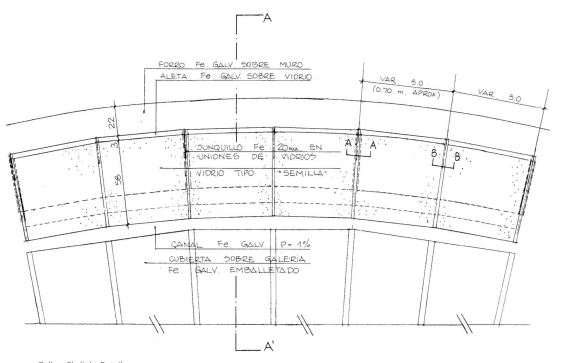

A

FORRO Fe. GALV. SOBRE MURO
ALETA Fe. GALV. SOBRE VIDRIO

VAR. 5.0
(0.70 m. APROX)
VAR. 5.0

22
3
58

JUNQUILLO Fe 20mm. EN
UNIONES DE VIDRIOS
VIDRIO TIPO "SEMILLA"

A   A
B   B

CANAL Fe. GALV. P= 1%
CUBIERTA SOBRE GALERIA
Fe. GALV. EMBALLETADO

A'

Gallery Skylight Details

House in San Damian Passage

Las Condes, Santiago, Chile

The site is located at the end of a natural passage. The best views and the best sunlight are in the opposite direction of the entrance to the terrain. Locating the house at the back of the site was the obvious choice. The sinuous entrance road also would serve as a walkway for pedestrians.

The house has two axes; the first crosses the width of the entire site. It consists of a one-level parrón with wooden beams, two children's bedrooms, bathrooms, and a kitchen. The second axis has two levels and is cut perpendicularly to the interior. It corresponds to the more public program of the double-height living room and the dining room. The parents' spaces are located above the dining room. The entrance hall—also of double height—is located at the intersection of the two axes, and has natural overhead light.

The disposition of the two axes of the house also serves to delimit the exterior spaces. The service patio and a patio with orange trees—which offers tranquil views to the dining room and children's den—are located at the back. Toward the front, however, the intersection of the axes was not allowed to visually cut the garden. By the same token, the living room has a triangular form which terminates at the chimney. This allows the front corridor and the children's bedrooms to embrace the garden. In its turn, the oblique direction of the living room windows orients its internal space to the north, which offers the most far-reaching views.

The thermal regulation of the house was carefully considered. The fronts facing toward the south are very hermetic, and in some cases they have a double wall. In front of the hanging windows toward the north, square membranes of wood are suspended. Through these, climbers of deciduous leaves will rise, fluctuating according to the seasons of the year. Furthermore, these membranes expand the virtual space of the living room, dining room, and main bedroom.

Above: View of the living room from the swimming pool.

Opposite Page: View from the exterior corridor toward the living room. The corridor is protected by a horizontal trellis, while the living room is protected by a vertical one. Both are now completely covered by creeper plants.

1. *Entrance Hall*
2. *Living Room*
3. *Dining Room*
4. *Kitchen*
5. *Service Quarters*
6. *Bedrooms*
7. *Family Room*
8. *Pool*
9. *Changing Rooms*

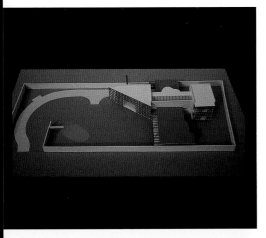

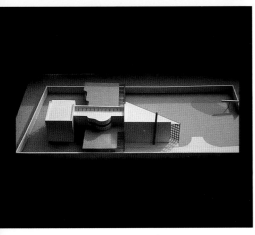

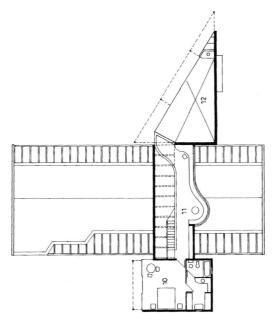

Second Floor Plan

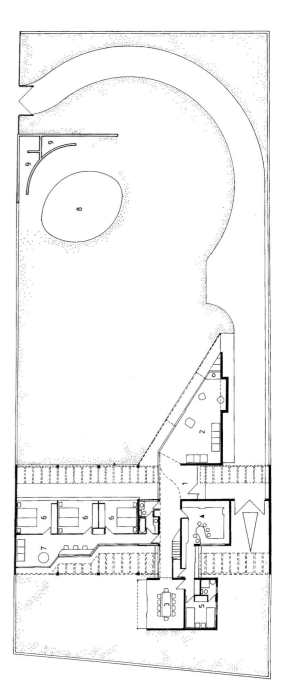

First Floor Plan

0 1   5 m

Left: *(Top) Sectional view of the triangular volume of the living room, taken from the drive. It also shows the vertical trellis that protects it. (Bottom) Views of horizontal and vertical trellises, with and without vegetation.*

Opposite Page: *Overhead views of the preliminary model.*

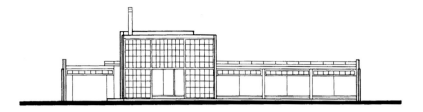

Northeast Elevation

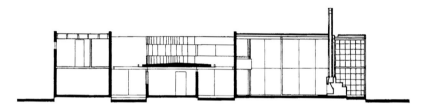

Transversal Section

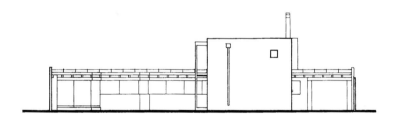

Southwest Elevation

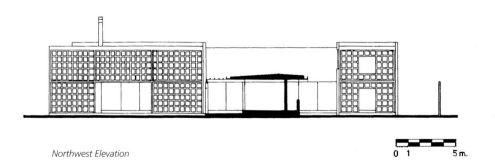

Northwest Elevation

0   1   5 m.

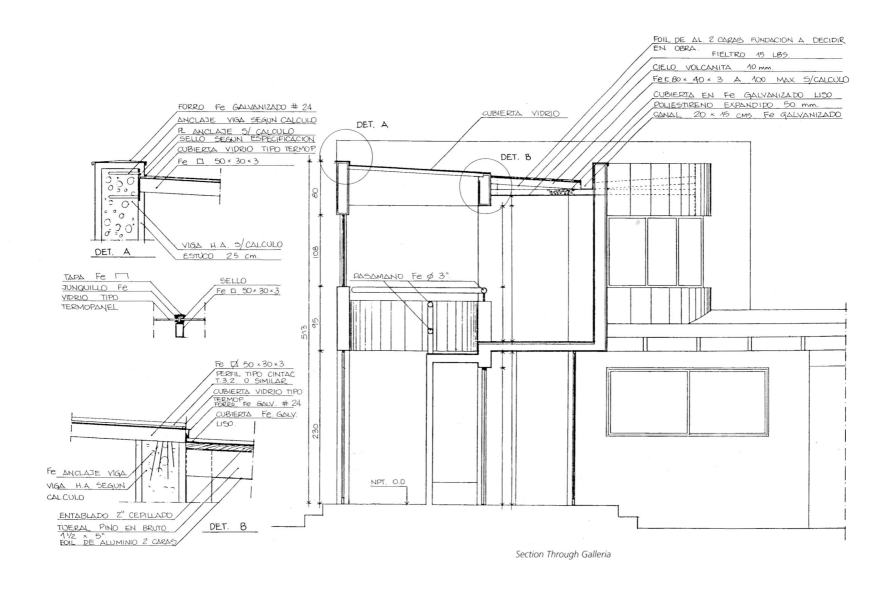

FOIL DE AL. 2 CARAS FUNDACION A DECIDIR
EN OBRA.
FIELTRO 15 LBS.
CIELO VOLCANITA 10 mm.
Fe ⊏ 80 × 40 × 3 A 100 MAX S/CALCULO
CUBIERTA EN Fe GALVANIZADO LISO
POLIESTIRENO EXPANDIDO 50 mm.
CANAL 20 × 15 CMS. Fe GALVANIZADO

FORRO Fe GALVANIZADO # 24
ANCLAJE VIGA SEGUN CALCULO
PL ANCLAJE S/ CALCULO
SELLO SEGUN ESPECIFICACION
CUBIERTA VIDRIO TIPO TERMOP.
Fe ◻ 50 × 30 × 3

CUBIERTA VIDRIO

DET. A

DET. B

VIGA H.A. S/CALCULO
ESTUCO 2.5 cm.

DET. A

TAPA Fe ⊓
JUNQUILLO Fe
VIDRIO TIPO
TERMOPANEL

SELLO
Fe ◻ 50 × 30 × 3

PASAMANO Fe ∅ 3"

Fe ◻ 50 × 30 × 3
PERFIL TIPO CINTAC
T.3.2. O SIMILAR
CUBIERTA VIDRIO TIPO
TERMOP.
FORRO Fe GALV. # 24
CUBIERTA Fe GALV.
LISO.

Fe ANCLAJE VIGA
VIGA H.A. SEGUN
CALCULO

ENTABLADO 2" CEPILLADO
TUERAL PINO EN BRUTO
1 1/2 × 5"
FOIL DE ALUMINIO 2 CARAS

DET. B

NPT. 0.0

80

108

513

95

230

Section Through Galleria

Left: *(Top) View of the living room from the second floor. (Bottom) Informal living room on the first floor, and kitchen.*

House on La Cumbre Street

Las Condes, Santiago, Chile

The terrain is located in the highest zone of a subdivision on the Manquehue (hill). The house required a special solution because the entrance is below the structure. Looking upwards, views can be had of the hill's summit and the northern sun; looking downwards, there are excellent panoramic views of the city, but without sunlight. The main problems, then, consisted of where to place the house and how to allow access to it.

To obtain the magnificent double view and profound sense of orientation, the house was set in the middle of the site. A roofed gallery with thermopanes divides the terrain and the house in two halves, giving sunlight to the southern part of the house where the changing of the time of day and the climate can be best appreciated. The public areas (the living room, dining room, and studies) face toward Santiago; the private areas (the bedrooms) face the summit and receive the northern sun.

The entrance is designed through a pathway that reveals the topographical characteristics and, simultaneously, offers diversity and surprise. From the parking area, a groove follows in a diagonal that actually penetrates into the earth. Formed by stone-containing walls, it becomes narrower and deeper as it progresses. Passing by a bridge that forms a threshold, the wall ultimately arrives at a high triangular patio with a waterfall and some rocks. Only the sky is visible at this point. At the bottom, the stairs of the entrance return over themselves. A white glass gallery lies just inside the entrance to the house, offering a spatial experience that is very different from the previous rocky, shady, and humid environment.

The entrance intersects with the gallery and gives rise to four patios. The two major patios (garden and bedroom) form one diagonal, and the two minor ones (study and service area) form another.

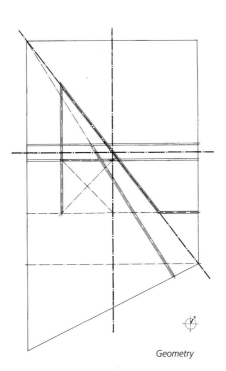

Geometry

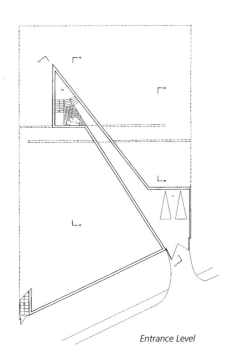

Entrance Level

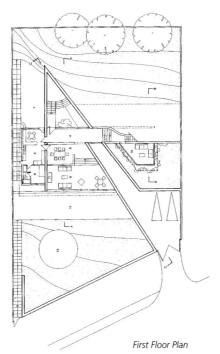

First Floor Plan

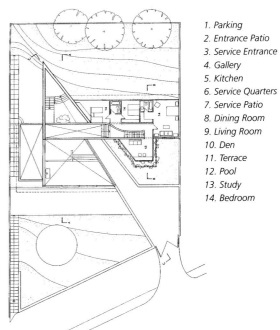

Second Floor Plan

1. Parking
2. Entrance Patio
3. Service Entrance
4. Gallery
5. Kitchen
6. Service Quarters
7. Service Patio
8. Dining Room
9. Living Room
10. Den
11. Terrace
12. Pool
13. Study
14. Bedroom

Left: *(Top) The wall facing the street also forms an elevated patio, from which one can view Santiago. The public areas of the dwelling lead on to this sight-seeing patio. (Bottom) Side view of the model. All of the bedrooms lead on to this sunny back patio and look over the Manquehue hill.*

Opposite Page: *The roofs follow the slant of the hillside. The pergola rests vertically on the edifice.*

Right: Overhead view of the model. One can
fully appreciate the geometry that dominates
the house.

Opposite Page: (Top) Aerial view of the house.
(Bottom) Detail of the triangular entrance patio
and its relation to the hallway with zenith
lighting.

In order to emphasize the topography, all the roofs of the house follow a continuous inclination parallel to the slope. Furthermore, the wood ceilings are convex, to accentuate the views. A wooden pergola makes a vertical counterpoint of the house. Inside, the parents' study is located below and the children's den above the pergola. Both offer views of Santiago. The plan of the house came to fruition in a strict geometrical layout.

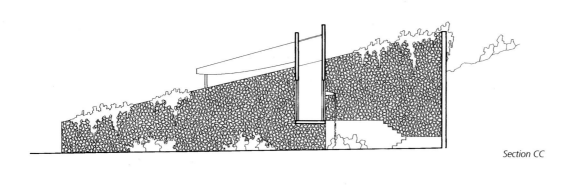

Section CC

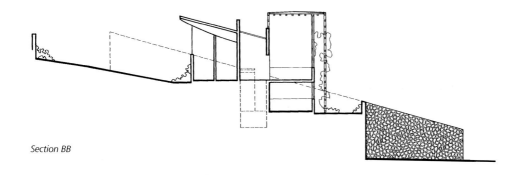

Section BB

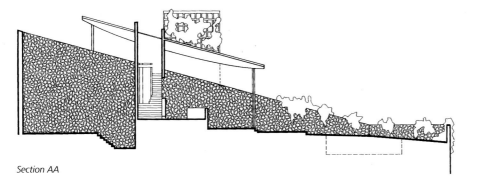

Section AA

CAMINO EL CONDOR

Bilbao-Uribe House

Las Condes, Santiago, Chile

Located on the lower slopes of San Cristobal Hill, the house affords spectacular views of Santiago and the mountains to the south and east. It also faces, from above, a new urbanization toward the west. But its saddle-like topography presented difficulties in merging the excellent views with good sunlight, access, and other aspects of the program.

The solution consisted of having a vehicular entrance at the upper-most portion of the terrain, in order to return toward a parking rotunda with panoramic views of the city and the mountains. The pedestrian entrance is located by a flight of stone stairs and grass arranged in the form of a "V" toward the entrance rotunda. This conical entrance has overhead natural lighting. The division toward the two wings of the house is also in a "V" shape. One of the wings of the "V" shape comprises the bedrooms facing the garden and the new development. The other, double-height wing faces toward Santiago through a large terrace. The conical entrance also contains a spiral stairway that rises toward the study and a game room, forming a balcony at the extremes of the dining room and living room.

A parrón protects the bedrooms from the western sun, and continues parallel to the wall that demarcates the entrance. It ultimately arrives at an open-air pergola.

Above: Observe the corridor that runs between the bedrooms and the garden. It continues with a trellis that ends in a pergola for taking meals outside.

Opposite Page: The geometry of the dwelling derives from the difficult relief of the terrain and from its position in relation to the sun. The "V"-shaped access concludes in the entrance rotunda, dividing the layout into two sectors. The public areas are toward the Santiago side. The bedrooms are toward the side exposed to the sun.

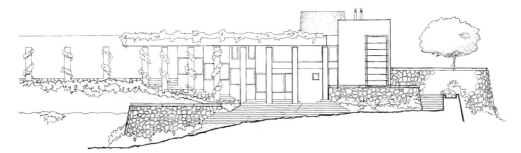

1. Entrance Hall
2. Bedroom
3. Service Quarters
4. Kitchen
5. Service Patio
6. Equipment Room
7. Dining Room
8. Living Room
9. Terrace
10. Pool
11. Study
12. Entrance Patio
13. Pergola
14. Vantage Point Terrace

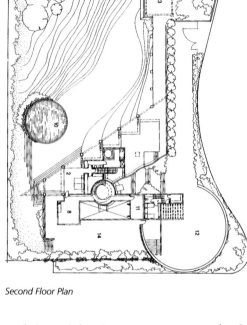

Second Floor Plan

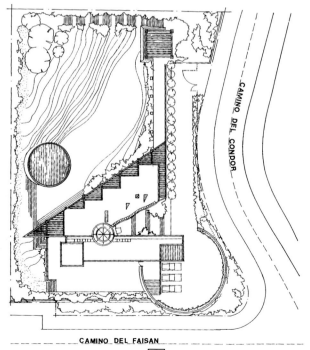

CAMINO DEL CONDOR

CAMINO DEL FAISAN

Site Plan

0 1 5 10 m.

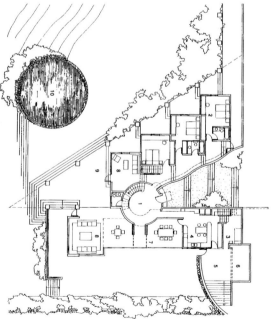

First Floor Plan

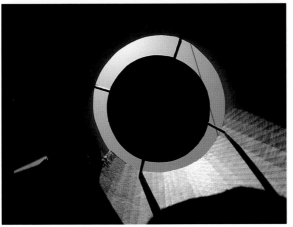

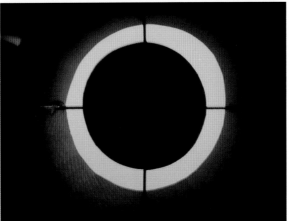

Left: (Top) View of the house and back garden with its pool and pergola. (Bottom) Zenith lighting of the entrance rotunda, with natural or golden light.

Opposite Page: Details of the entrance rotunda.

Right: *Different aerial views of the house.*

Opposite Page: *(Top) The stone wall harbors a considerable terrace that looks down on Santiago. (Bottom) From the parking rotunda, Santiago is visible.*

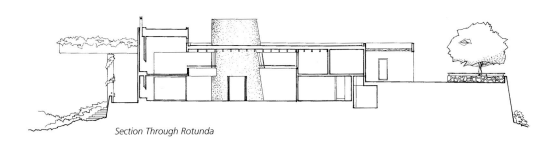

Section Through Rotunda

Section Through Dining Room-Living Room

South Elevation

East Elevation

Selected Buildings and Projects

House in Pirque (Version I)
Cruceral, Pirque, Chile

Principal Architects: Enrique Browne, Ricardo Judson
Assistant Architects: Jorge Campos, Enrique Merino, Veronica Celedón
Site: 55,555 sq. ft. (5,000 sq. mt.)
Building: 1,355 sq. ft. (122 sq. mt.)
Date of Design: 1984

House in San Damian Passage
Las Condes, Santiago, Chile

Principal Architects: Enrique Browne, Eduardo San Martin, Patricio Wenborne
Structural Engineers: Harmut Vogel and Rodrigo Mujica
Site: 17,333 sq. ft. (1,560 sq. mt.)
Building: 3,288 sq. ft. (296 sq. mt.)
Date of Design: 1986
Construction Completed: 1987

Houses on Charles Hamilton Street
Las Condes, Santiago, Chile

Assistant Architects: Roberto Fernández, Alex Moreno, Bernardo Onfray, Vicente Rodríguez
Structural Engineer: Del Sol, Vogel and Mujica
Site: 30,000 sq. ft. (2,700 sq. mt.) each one
Building: 1,555 sq. ft. (140 sq. mt.)
Date of Design: 1974
Construction Completed: 1975

Summer House in Zapallar
Zapallar, Chile

Assistant Architects: Bernardo Onfray, Jorge Campos, Enrique Merino, Veronica Celedón
Site: 10,000 sq. ft. (900 sq. mt.)
Building: 888 sq. ft. (80 sq. mt.)
Date of Design: 1984

House in Pirque (Version II)
Cruceral, Pirque, Chile

Principal Architects: Enrique Browne, Guillermo Geisse, Ricardo Judson
Structural Engineer: Rodrigo Mujica
Site: 55,555 sq. ft. (5,000 sq. mt.)
Building: 1,044 sq. ft. (94 sq. mt.)
Date of Design: 1986
Construction Completed: 1987

House on La Cumbre Street
Las Condes, Santiago, Chile

Assistant Architects: Jorge Campos, Isabel Perelló, Ivan Hernández
Site: 13,155 sq. ft. (1,184 sq. mt.)
Building: 3,111 sq. ft. (280 sq. mt.)
Date of Design: 1989

House on Paul Harris Street
Las Condes, Santiago, Chile

Assistant Architects: Ricardo Judson, Manuel Claro, Ricardo Cruz
Structural Engineer: Rodrigo Mujica
Site: 23,333 sq. ft. (2,100 sq. mt)
Building: 4,444 sq. ft. (400 sq. mt.)
Date of Design: 1980
Construction Completed: 1982

House on La Fuente Street
Las Condes, Santiago, Chile

Principal Architects: Enrique Browne, Ricardo Judson
Site: 15,555 sq. ft. (1,400 sq. mt.)
Building: 2,755 sq. ft. (248 sq. mt.)
Date of Design: 1984
Construction Completed: 1985–1986

Snail House
Las Condes, Santiago, Chile

Assistant Architects: Jorge Campos, Ricardo Cruz
Structural Engineers: Harmut Vogel and Rodrigo Mujica
Site: 9,000 sq. ft. (810 sq. mt.)
Building: 2,866 sq. ft. (258 sq. mt.)
Date of Design: 1985
Construction Completed: 1987

Bilbao-Uribe House
Las Condes, Santiago, Chile

Principal Architects: Enrique Browne, Ricardo Judson
Assistant Architects: Isabel Perelló, Jaime Irarrazaval
Structural Engineers: Harmut Vogel and Rodrigo Mujica
Site: 32,222 sq. ft. (2,900 sq. mt.)
Building: 5,233 sq. ft. (471 sq. mt.)
Date of Design: 1991

The firm Enrique Browne & Associates, Architects, was founded in 1990 after its principal parted from his previous associates, Eduardo San Martin and Patricio Wenborne. He was also partners with Ricardo Judson for two years. The current firm has fluctuated between ten and twenty people, depending on the project load.

Enrique Browne received his Architecture degree in 1965 and a Masters in Urbanism in 1968. Both degrees were conferred by Universidad Católica de Chile with "Highest Honors." From 1969 to 1971, he was granted a fellowship by the Ford Foundation to complete advanced studies at the Joint Center for Urban Studies (MIT and Harvard University), the Joint Unit for Planning Research (London University), and the Japan Center for Area Development Research.

Upon his return to Chile, he became professor at the Center for Urban Studies and was later unanimously named Secretary General of the Universidad Católica. In 1974 he began to devote himself entirely to architecture. His first work, Houses On Charles Hamilton Street, received "First Prize" in the II Architectural Biennial of Santiago, Chile. He was subsequently awarded fifteen prizes and honorable mentions in other Biennials of different countries, including "Steel Cube" at the II Buenos Aires International Biennial, "Silver Medal" at the World Biennial of Architecture in Sofia (Bulgaria), and another "First Prize" at the X Architectural Biennial of Santiago, Chile.

Parallel to his professional activities, Enrique Browne has maintained his interest in urban and architectural research. As fellow of the Social Science Research Council (1977) and the Guggenheim Foundation (1983), he has written three books, including *Otra Arquitectura en América Latina* (Ediciones G. Gili, México, 1988), and co-authored five others. He has also written more than fifty essays. He has given numerous conferences in Latin America, the United States., and in Europe. His works have been published nearly 100 times in specialized magazines in diverse countries, including two monographs. The last is *Enrique Browne, Architect, Works 1974-1994* (Ediciones ARO, Santiago, Chile, 1995).

The size and scope of his works have grown over the years. His first projects were preferably private homes, while in later years he has worked more on office buildings (Tajamar, Consorcio, Sonda, and Pioneer), public buildings (Twelve Courts), and healthcare facilities (Clinic of the "Mutual de Seguridad" of the Chilean Construction Association), among others. Nevertheless, he has always maintained his interest in single-family houses. With responsive clients, this area offers great possibilities for experimentation, and often the results can be used in major works.

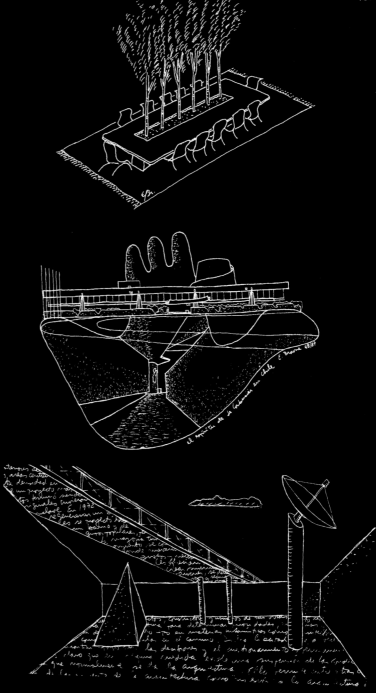

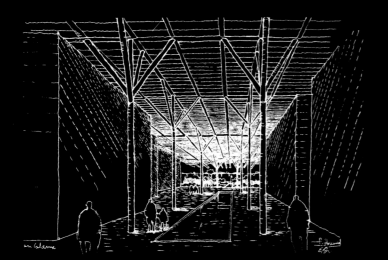

Photographic Credits

Alfonso Barrios

Snail House

Enrique Browne

Houses on Charles Hamilton Street

House on Paul Harris Street

House on La Cumbre Street

Bilbao-Uribe House

Carmen Dominguez

House on Paul Harris Street

Luis Poirot

Houses on Charles Hamilton Street

House on Paul Harris Street

House on La Fuente Street

House in Pirque (Version II)

House in San Damian Passage

Guy Wenbourne

House in Pirque (Version I)

Summer House in Zapallar

House on La Cumbre Street

Bilbao-Uribe House